JOURNEYS

Benchmark and Unit Tests
Teacher's Edition

Grade 1

Printed in the U.S.A.

ISBN 13: 978-0-547-31873-8
ISBN 10: 0-547-31873-2

1 2 3 4 5 6 7 8 9 10 0982 18 17 16 15 14 13 12 11 10

HOUGHTON MIFFLIN HARCOURT
School Publishers

Contents

Introduction 1–3

Documents for Scoring Tests

Answer Key, Units 1–6 6–14

Writing Rubric and Sample Written Responses

Writing Rubric 17

Sample Written Responses 18–21

Blackline Masters for Recording Test Performance

Test Record Form 25

Performance Summary 27–28

Introduction

Overview: The Benchmark and Unit Tests

As you use the Houghton Mifflin Harcourt *Journeys* instructional program, you have a rich array of materials to foster children's achievement week-by-week and unit-by-unit. The assessment materials supplement the *Journeys* program, offering you many ways to track children's progress and adjust your instructional focus to meet their needs.

The Weekly Tests and the Periodic Assessments (Checklists and Fluency Tests) show achievement in specific program skill strands throughout a unit. At the *end* of each unit, there is one test to offer you a broader picture of achievement: a Benchmark Test or a Unit Test.

Benchmark Tests   The Benchmark Tests are given three times a year, at the end of Units 1, 3, and 5. These tests focus on the key reading/language arts skills that have been taught to date. The Unit 1 Benchmark Test draws upon selected skills from that unit as well as other skills that indicate general reading achievement. The Benchmark Tests in Units 3 and 5 are summative, drawing upon skills that have been taught in the program up to the point of administration along with other indicators of reading progress.

Each Benchmark Test has four sections. The **Reading** section assesses comprehension and vocabulary strategies. The **Phonics** section assesses phonics skills in context. The **Revising and Editing** section (Units 4–6 only) draws upon the grammar and spelling skills taught to date. The **Written Composition** section provides a writing prompt, reflecting the modes, forms, and skills taught to date.

Test items and test formats are representative of the items found on state tests, providing essential practice in test-taking strategies. In addition, the Answer Keys correlate the items to appropriate strands in the Teacher's Edition, to help you plan re-teaching lessons and extra practice as needed.

Unit Tests   Alternating with the Benchmark Tests, the Unit Tests assess progress on the skills taught in Units 2, 4, and 6. Unlike the Benchmark Tests, the Unit Tests are not cumulative but provide a focus on the skills in a particular unit. The results help you to confirm scores on the Weekly Tests and to pinpoint skills for re-teaching or challenge lessons. The Unit Test sections **(Reading, Phonics, Revising and Editing, Written Composition)** and item formats also provide practice with test-taking strategies, and the Answer Keys correlate the items to instructional lessons in the program.

Administering the Tests

The Benchmark and Unit Tests are group-administered. Although children can read the passages and answer choices, some *questions* contain non-decodable words that pose a challenge. For that reason, important directions for administering the tests appear in the "To the teacher" notes at the bottom of the first page in each test section.

For each test, the four sections may be given in different sittings. For **Written Composition,** coach children to refer to the tips in the "Remember—You Should . . ." box that accompanies the writing prompt.

Scoring the Tests

The **Reading, Phonics,** and **Revising and Editing** subtests consist of multiple-choice items. Correct the tests using the Answer Keys on pages 6–14 of this book, placing a check mark next to each correct response on the student page. Each correct response is worth one point. Duplicate a Test Record Form (page 25) for each child and enter the scores in the Student Score column. This form will allow you to track a child's performance across the year.

If you require a percentage score for each test to help in assigning grades, apply the formula in the optional Percent Correct column and record that score.

For **Written Composition,** score each child's writing by using the rubric on page 17 of this book and enter the score on the Test Record Form. As a guide for using the rubric, some sample student papers that represent different scores are provided on pages 18–21.

Interpreting the Results

Consider each child's scores on the Test Record Form. Children who achieve an Acceptable Score (indicated on the form) or higher are most likely ready to proceed with the next unit. You may want to look at class scores across each subtest to see if there are specific skills you should reinforce with the whole class in the next unit.

For struggling children, duplicate the Performance Summary on pages 27–28. Circle the item numbers answered incorrectly on each subtest and compare them to the corresponding skills indicated on the Answer Keys. Look for patterns among the errors to help you decide which skills need re-teaching and more practice. To assess progress after re-teaching, re-administer an appropriate Weekly Test or go over errors on the Benchmark or Unit Test and have the children explain which responses are correct. Consider intervention for children who still have a wide array of errors.

Summary

The broad picture of reading/writing achievement offered by the Benchmark and Unit Tests helps you in three important ways:

- The tests show you how children combine the skills from the Weekly Tests and apply them to new selections.
- Children's performance helps you tailor your instruction to meet their needs.
- The formats and skills on the Benchmark and Unit Tests prepare children with important test-taking strategies.

Use the options in the *Journeys* assessment materials to verify progress and enhance your teaching throughout the year.

Documents
for
Scoring Tests

Answer Key
Unit 1, Benchmark Test

Item Number	Correct Answer	Unit, Lesson, Program Skill
		Reading
1	**C** sad	U1L2: Comprehension: Understanding Characters
2	**A** pal	U1L5: High-Frequency Words
3	**B** go find	U1L2: High-Frequency Words
4	**A** Pam pets Tom.	U1L3: Comprehension: Sequence of Events
5	**B** Pam looks at Tom and Sam.	U1L3: Comprehension: Sequence of Events
6	**A** picture: children playing tag	U1L2: Vocabulary Strategy: Context Clues
7	**A** not sad	U1L2: Comprehension: Understanding Characters
8	**B** cat	U1L4: Vocabulary Strategy: Alphabetical Order
9	**C** picture: man	U1L2: High-Frequency Words
10	**B** The pigs run to it.	U1L3: Comprehension: Sequence of Events
11	**C** what the hens look like	U1L4: Comprehension: Text and Graphic Features
12	**B** He pops up the lid.	U1L3: Comprehension: Sequence of Events
13	**C** runs	U1L1: Vocabulary Strategy: Classification/Categorization of Words: Actions
14	**B** lots	U1L5: High-Frequency Words
15	**C** He has many jobs to do.	U1L1: Comprehension: Main Idea
		Reading: Phonics
16	**A** cat	U1L1: Phonics: Short *a*
17	**C** wig	U1L2: Phonics: Short *i*
18	**B** It	U1L2: Phonics: Short *i*
19	**C** fox	U1L3: Phonics: Short *o*
20	**B** hops	U1L3: Phonics: Inflection -*s*
21	**A** can	U1L1: Phonics: Short *a*
22	**C** fun	U1L5: Phonics: Short *u*
23	**B** hot	U1L3: Phonics: Short *o*
24	**A** get	U1L4: Phonics: Short *e*
25	**A** fan	U1L1: Phonics: Short *a*
		Writing: Written Composition
	See rubric on page 17.	U1L1: Writing About Us

Unit 2, Unit Test

Item Number	Correct Answer	Unit, Lesson, Program Skill
		Reading
1	**B** picture: classroom	U2L10: Comprehension: Story Structure
2	**C** picture: girl eating	U2L10: High-Frequency Words
3	**A** Kim does not have a snack.	U2L6: Comprehension: Understanding Characters
4	**C** picture: girl drawing	U2L9: High-Frequency Words
5	**B** got	U2L6: Vocabulary Strategy: Classification/Categorization of Words: Actions
6	**C** Kim lets Jan have some pens.	U2L8: Comprehension: Sequence of Events
7	**A** Now	U2L8: Vocabulary Strategy: Classification/Categorization of Words: Time
8	**A** She helps.	U2L6: Comprehension: Understanding Characters
9	**A** picture: cat	U2L9: Comprehension: Text and Graphic Features
10	**C** picture: squirrel	U2L7: High-Frequency Words
11	**B** many	U2L10: Vocabulary Strategy: Synonyms
12	**A** big	U2L9: Vocabulary Strategy: Antonyms
13	**C** We see you get cat bits in a bag.	U2L9: Comprehension: Text and Graphic Features
14	**B** Make a soft bed.	U2L7: Comprehension: Details
15	**C** A cat would like a friend.	U2L7: Comprehension: Details
		Reading: Phonics
16	**B** plan	U2L8: Phonics: Clusters with *l*
17	**C** trip	U2L7: Phonics: Clusters with *r*
18	**B** back	U2L6: Phonics: Final -*ck*
19	**C** will	U2L6: Phonics: Double Final Consonants
20	**A** lift	U2L10: Phonics: Final Clusters
21	**B** stack	U2L6: Phonics: Final -*ck*
22	**A** strap	U2L9: Phonics: 2- and 3-letter Clusters with *s*
23	**C** drop	U2L7: Phonics: Clusters with *r*
24	**A** clock	U2L8: Phonics: Clusters with *l*
25	**B** jump	U2L10: Phonics: Final Clusters
		Writing: Written Composition
	See rubric on page 17.	U2L10: Write to Describe

Unit 3, Benchmark Test

Item Number	Correct Answer	Unit, Lesson, Program Skill
		Reading
1	**A** She will get a cat.	U2L6: Comprehension: Understanding Characters
2	**B** blue	U3L11: Vocabulary Strategy: Classification/Categorization of Words: Colors
3	**A** not up	U3L13: High-Frequency Words
4	**A** A cat bumps her leg.	U3L13: Comprehension: Cause and Effect
5	**C** have fun	U1L1: High-Frequency Words
6	**A** The cat is white and soft.	U3L14: Comprehension: Conclusions
7	**A** Dad nods.	U3L12: Comprehension: Sequence of Events
8	**B** grin	U1L2: Vocabulary Strategy: Context Clues
9	**C** picture: water	U3L11: High-Frequency Words
10	**B** fins and scales	U2L7: Comprehension: Details
11	**A** two	U3L14: Vocabulary Strategy: Classification/Categorization of Words: Numbers
12	**B** how the frog hides	U2L9: Comprehension: Text and Graphic Features
13	**C** picture: boy eating	U2L10: High-Frequency Words
14	**B** Plants and animals both live in a pond.	U1L1: Comprehension: Main Idea
15	**B** to tell what is in a pond	U3L11: Comprehension: Author's Purpose
		Reading: Phonics
16	**C** bath	U3L11: Phonics: Digraph *th*
17	**B** didn't	U3L13: Phonics: Contractions with *'s, n't*
18	**C** catch	U3L12: Phonics: Digraphs *ch, tch*
19	**C** tub	U1L5: Phonics: Short *u*
20	**A** He's	U3L13: Phonics; Contractions with *'s, n't*
21	**C** whine	U3L13: Phonics: Digraphs *sh, wh, ph*
22	**A** shake	U3L14: Phonics: Long *a* (CVCe)
23	**C** splash	U2L9: Phonics: 2- and 3-Letter Clusters with *s*
24	**B** drip	U2L7: Phonics: Clusters with *r*
25	**B** wet	U1L4: Phonics: Short *e*
		Writing: Written Composition
	See rubric on page 17.	U3L12: Write to Inform

Unit 4, Unit Test

Item Number	Correct Answer	Unit, Lesson, Program Skill
		Reading
1	**A** It is raining.	U4L20: Comprehension: Cause and Effect
2	**A** not new	U4L20: High-Frequency Words
3	**A** Mom opens the box.	U3L12: Comprehension: Sequence of Events
4	**C** stay inside	U4L17: Comprehension: Compare and Contrast
5	**A** take	U4L16: High-Frequency Words
6	**B** Mom played with them both.	U4L17: Comprehension: Compare and Contrast
7	**C** little	U4L19: Vocabulary Strategy: Synonyms
8	**B** makes a song	U4L18: Vocabulary Strategy: Multiple-Meaning Words
9	**C** You see how mail gets to you.	U4L16: Comprehension: Main Idea and Details
10	**A** a box to put mail in	U4L20: Vocabulary Strategy: Compound Words
11	**B** a code for where someone lives	U4L16: Comprehension: Main Idea and Details
12	**A** truck	U4L17: Vocabulary Strategy: Classification/Categorization of Words: Transportation
13	**A** to tell who it is for	U4L19: Comprehension: Conclusions
14	**B** take to a new place	U4L16: High-Frequency Words
15	**B** to tell facts about mail	U4L18: Comprehension: Author's Purpose
16	**A** sleepover	U4L20: Vocabulary Strategy: Compound Words
		Reading: Phonics
17	**A** rain	U4L18: Phonics: Vowel Pairs *ai, ay*
18	**B** seek	U4L17: Phonics: Vowel Pairs *ee, ea*
19	**A** close	U4L16: Phonics: Long *o*
20	**B** huge	U4L16: Phonics: Long *u*
21	**C** these	U4L17: Phonics: Long *e*
22	**A** I'll	U4L18: Phonics: Contractions *'ll, 'd*
23	**C** head	U4L20: Phonics: Short Vowel /e/*ea*
24	**B** groaned	U4L19: Phonics: Vowel Pairs *oa, ow*
25	**B** You're	U4L19: Phonics: Contractions *'ve, 're*

Unit 4, Unit Test continued

Item Number	Correct Answer	Unit, Lesson, Program Skill
	**Writing: Revising and Editing**	
1	**C** tri	U4L17: Spelling: Long *e*
2	**C** mother's	U4L18: Grammar: Names of Months, Days, Holidays
3	**A** what	U4L16: Grammar: Writing Questions
4	**A** May 10, 2009	U4L18: Grammar: Commas in Dates
5	**B** under	U4L20: Grammar: Prepositions and Prepositional Phrases
6	**A** it	U4L17: Grammar: Writing Statements and Questions
7	**B** gives	U4L19: Grammar: Future Using *will*
8	**A** go	U4L19: Grammar: Future Tense
9	**B** grai	U4L19: Spelling: Vowel Pairs *oa, ow*
10	**B** ?	U4L17: Grammar: Statement or Question?
	**Writing: Written Composition**	
	See rubric on page 17.	U4L20: Write to Narrate

Unit 5, Benchmark Test

Item Number	Correct Answer	Unit, Lesson, Program Skill
		**Reading**
1	**A** She wants a kite.	U5L21: Comprehension: Story Structure
2	**A** have a plan	U3L12: High-Frequency Words
3	**C** a ride that has wheels	U4L17: High-Frequency Words
4	**B** Carl gets the lunch bag.	U5L24: Comprehension: Sequence of Events
5	**A** fixed	U1L1: Vocabulary Strategy: Classification/Categorization of Words: Actions
6	**B** Joy runs with it.	U5L24: Comprehension: Sequence of Events
7	**A** glad	U5L25: Comprehension: Understanding Characters
8	**B** family	U5L23: Vocabulary Strategy: Classification/Categorization of Words: Family
9	**A** It will tell about ants.	U2L9: Comprehension: Text and Graphic Features
10	**C** the part that is up	U5L24: Vocabulary Strategy: Multiple-Meaning Words
11	**C** not many	U2L7: High-Frequency Words
12	**A** to lay eggs	U2L7: Comprehension: Details
13	**C** a very young animal	U5L22: High-Frequency Words
14	**B** Ants have jobs that help their family.	U1L1: Comprehension: Main Idea
15	**B** to tell facts about ants	U4L18: Comprehension: Author's Purpose
		**Reading: Phonics**
16	**A** steps	U1L4: Phonics: Short *e*
17	**B** need	U4L17: Phonics: Vowel Pairs *ee, ea*
18	**C** that	U3L11: Phonics: Digraph *th*
19	**B** smooth	U5L24: Phonics: Vowel Digraphs/Spelling Patterns *oo, ou, ew*
20	**C** soil	U5L25: Phonics: Vowel Combinations *oi, oy, au, aw*
21	**A** farm	U5L21: Phonics: *r*-Controlled Vowel *ar*
22	**A** paint	U4L18: Phonics: Vowel Pairs *ai, ay*
23	**A** face	U3L14: Phonics: Soft *c, g, dge*
24	**B** isn't	U3L13: Phonics: Contractions with *'s, n't*
25	**B** long	U4L17: Phonics: Final *ng, nk*

Unit 5, Benchmark Test continued

Item Number	Correct Answer	Unit, Lesson, Program Skill
		Writing: Revising and Editing
1	**A** will	U4L19: Grammar: Future Using *will*
2	**A** Mom and I	U5L22: Grammar: The Pronoun *I*
3	**A** dod	U1L1: Spelling: Short *a*
4	**B** ?	U4L17: Grammar: Statement or Question?
5	**C** blue	U1L5: Grammar: Adjectives for Color
6	**B** were	U3L15: Grammar: The Verb *be*
7	**A** her	U5L23: Grammar: Possessive Pronouns
8	**C** toy	U2L9: Grammar: Singular and Plural Nouns
9	**A** going	U4L19: Grammar: Future Tense
10	**B** nat	U2L8: Spelling: Short *o*
		Writing: Written Composition
	See rubric on page 17.	U5L25: Write to Narrate

Unit 6, Unit Test

Item Number	Correct Answer	Unit, Lesson, Program Skill
		Reading
1	**B** at a pond	U6L28: Comprehension: Story Structure
2	**C** on a sunny day	U6L28: Comprehension: Story Structure
3	**B** liked a lot	U6L30: High-Frequency Words
4	**B** Fred can swim.	U6L26: Comprehension: Compare and Contrast
5	**A** feelings	U6L27: Vocabulary Strategy: Classification/Categorization of Words: Emotions
6	**B** close to	U6L27: High-Frequency Words
7	**A** It is easy.	U6L26: Vocabulary Strategy: Figurative Language (Idioms)
8	**C** glad, cool	U6L30: Comprehension: Understanding Characters
9	**B** a sailboat	U6L27: Comprehension: Text and Graphic Features
10	**A** get in and go	U6L28: Vocabulary Strategy: Homographs
11	**A** not like	U6L29: Vocabulary Strategy: Prefix *un-*
12	**B** The sail blocks it.	U6L29: Comprehension: Cause and Effect
13	**A** big	U6L28: High-Frequency Words
14	**B** They show what it looks like.	U6L27: Comprehension: Text and Graphic Features
15	**B** It makes the sailboat go faster.	U6L29: Comprehension: Cause and Effect
		Reading: Phonics
16	**C** light	U6L28: Phonics: Long *i* Spelling Patterns *igh, y, ie*
17	**B** hopped	U6L26: Phonics: Base Words/Inflections *-ed, -ing* (CVCe, CVC)
18	**C** quickly	U6L29: Phonics: Suffixes *-ful, -ly, -y*
19	**A** happy	U6L26: Phonics: Long *e* Spelling Patterns *y, ie*
20	**B** stable	U6L30: Phonics: Syllabication (CV)
21	**C** shy	U6L28: Phonics: Long *i* Spelling Patterns *igh, y, ie*
22	**A** nicest	U6L28: Phonics: Base Words/Inflections *-ed, -ing, -er, -est, -es*
23	**B** unsafe	U6L30: Phonics: Prefixes *un-, re-*
24	**C** so	U6L29: Phonics: Long Vowel Spelling Patterns *a, e, i, o, u*
25	**B** purple	U6L27: Phonics: Syllable *-le*

Unit 6, Unit Test continued

Item Number	Correct Answer	Unit, Lesson, Program Skill
	**Writing: Revising and Editing**	
1	**C** pai	U6L28: Spelling: Spelling Patterns *igh, y, ie*
2	**C** tawble	U6L30: Spelling: Syllables CV
3	**A** sweet	U6L28: Grammar: Adjectives for Taste and Smell
4	**B** ?	U6L27: Grammar: Question or Exclamation?
5	**C** biggest	U6L30: Grammar: Adjectives with *er* and *est*
6	**C** hard	U6L28: Grammar: Adjectives for Sound and Texture
7	**A** here	U6L29: Grammar: Adverbs for How and Where
8	**A** .	U6L27: Grammar: Three Kinds of Sentences
9	**B** very	U6L29: Grammar: Adverbs for When and How Much
10	**C** !	U6L26: Grammar: What is an Exclamation?
	**Writing: Written Composition**	
	See rubric on page 17.	U6L30: Write to Respond

Writing Rubric
and
Sample Written Responses

Writing Rubric

	Focus/Ideas	Organization	Voice	Word Choice	Sentence Fluency	Conventions
4	Adheres to the topic, is interesting, has a sense of completeness. Ideas are well developed.	Ideas and details are clearly presented and well organized.	Connects with the reader in a unique, personal way.	Includes vivid verbs, strong adjectives, specific nouns.	Includes a variety of complete sentences that flow smoothly, naturally.	Shows a strong command of grammar, spelling, capitalization, punctuation.
3	Mostly adheres to the topic, is somewhat interesting, has a sense of completeness. Ideas are adequately developed.	Ideas and details are mostly clear and generally organized.	Generally connects with reader in a way that is personal and sometimes unique.	Includes some vivid verbs, strong adjectives, specific nouns.	Includes some variety of mostly complete sentences. Some parts flow smoothly, naturally.	Shows a good command of grammar, spelling, capitalization, punctuation.
2	Does not always adhere to the topic, has some sense of completeness. Ideas are superficially developed.	Ideas and details are not always clear or organized. There is some wordiness or repetition.	Connects somewhat with reader. Sounds somewhat personal, but not unique.	Includes mostly simple nouns and verbs, and may have a few adjectives.	Includes mostly simple sentences, some of which are incomplete.	Some errors in grammar, spelling, capitalization, punctuation.
1	Does not adhere to the topic, has no sense of completeness. Ideas are vague.	Ideas and details are not organized. Wordiness or repetition hinders meaning.	Does not connect with reader. Does not sound personal or unique.	Includes only simple nouns and verbs, some inaccurate. Writing is not descriptive.	Sentences do not vary. Incomplete sentences hinder meaning.	Frequent errors in grammar, spelling, capitalization, punctuation.

Sample Written Responses: Scores 4–1

Use these model responses, scored 4–1, to guide your own scoring of children's responses to the writing prompts.

Sample prompt: Write a story about a time when you helped a friend.

Score 4   This story adheres to the topic and includes a clear beginning, middle, and ending. The writer uses words and phrases that connect with the reader. The writer also has a strong command of conventions; the misspelled words are challenging to spell, and errors do not interfere with meaning.

A time I helped my friend was at a.r. time on a computer. First I read the sentence on the computer. Then I read the questions. Next he picked a anwear. Finally he said "thank you". I said "your welcome". He got a 100% because I helped him. Now he is my best friend. now we will never stop friend ship.

Score 3   This story, while brief, mostly adheres to the topic. Most ideas are clear and developed with specific details. The writer uses some unique words and phrases to connect with the reader. The writer shows a fair command of conventions, attempting phonetic spelling of more challenging words.

One day me and my frend were on the bicicly. We were rasing. Then he feld of hes bicicly. And he got hert. I piced up hes bicicly and I coud hes dad for help. I os piced hes bicicly up.

Score 2 This story adheres to the topic, but ideas are listed and not developed. The writer attempts to connect with the reader, but ends up using repetitive language. The writer shows a command of most conventions, but incomplete sentences detract from meaning.

A time I helped my
friend. Was...
When she couldn't
tie her shoes.
And when she got
stuckk on the
Monkey bars. And
When she couldn't
get on the Monkey
bars. And When she
had a splinter.

Score 1 This story does not adhere to the topic. Ideas are unclear and not organized, with little or no development. The writer does not connect with the reader. Errors in conventions interfere with meaning.

I have 2 frinbs I play with them and I tack with them We acwese have fun We bo everythcing toogether

Blackline Masters
for
Recording Test Performance

Test Record Form

> **See the Answer Key for item analysis, including specific skills tested.**
> **For struggling children, use the Performance Summary to determine skills for reteaching.**

Unit 1 Benchmark Test Date Administered _____	Possible Score	Acceptable Score	Student Score	Percent Correct (%) (Optional)
Reading	15	12		Student Score × 6.67 = %
Reading: Phonics	10	8		Student Score × 10 = %
Writing: Written Composition	4	3		

Unit 2 Unit Test Date Administered _____	Possible Score	Acceptable Score	Student Score	Percent Correct (%) (Optional)
Reading	15	12		Student Score × 6.67 = %
Reading: Phonics	10	8		Student Score × 10 = %
Writing: Written Composition	4	3		

Unit 3 Benchmark Test Date Administered _____	Possible Score	Acceptable Score	Student Score	Percent Correct (%) (Optional)
Reading	15	12		Student Score × 6.67 = %
Reading: Phonics	10	8		Student Score × 10 = %
Writing: Written Composition	4	3		

Unit 4 Unit Test Date Administered _____	Possible Score	Acceptable Score	Student Score	Percent Correct (%) (Optional)
Reading	15	12		Student Score × 6.67 = %
Reading: Phonics	10	8		Student Score × 10 = %
Writing: Revising and Editing	10	8		Student Score × 10 = %
Writing: Written Composition	4	3		

Unit 5 Benchmark Test Date Administered _____	Possible Score	Acceptable Score	Student Score	Percent Correct (%) (Optional)
Reading	15	12		Student Score × 6.67 = %
Reading: Phonics	10	8		Student Score × 10 = %
Writing: Revising and Editing	10	8		Student Score × 10 = %
Writing: Written Composition	4	3		

Unit 6 Unit Test Date Administered _____	Possible Score	Acceptable Score	Student Score	Percent Correct (%) (Optional)
Reading	15	12		Student Score × 6.67 = %
Reading: Phonics	10	8		Student Score × 10 = %
Writing: Revising and Editing	10	8		Student Score × 10 = %
Writing: Written Composition	4	3		

Student Name _____

Performance Summary

> For struggling children, copy this form and circle the items answered incorrectly. In the third column record the specific skills for reteaching, using the item analysis on the Answer Key.

Unit 1 Benchmark Test   Date Administered _____

Reading Skills Performance		
Skill	**Items**	**Skills for Reteaching**
Comprehension Skills	1, 4, 5, 7, 10, 11, 12, 15	
High-Frequency Words	2, 3, 9, 14	
Vocabulary Strategies	6, 8, 13	
Phonics	16, 17, 18, 19, 20, 21, 22, 23, 24, 25	
Writing Performance		
Skill	**Items**	**Skills for Reteaching**
Writing Form	Writing Prompt	

Unit 2 Unit Test   Date Administered _____

Reading Skills Performance		
Skill	**Items**	**Skills for Reteaching**
Comprehension Skills	1, 3, 6, 8, 9, 13, 14, 15	
High-Frequency Words	2, 4, 10	
Vocabulary Strategies	5, 7, 11, 12	
Phonics	16, 17, 18, 19, 20, 21, 22, 23, 24, 25	
Writing Performance		
Skill	**Items**	**Skills for Reteaching**
Writing Form	Writing Prompt	

Unit 3 Benchmark Test   Date Administered _____

Reading Skills Performance		
Skill	**Items**	**Skills for Reteaching**
Comprehension Skills	1, 4, 6, 7, 10, 12, 14, 15	
High-Frequency Words	3, 5, 9, 13	
Vocabulary Strategies	2, 8, 11	
Phonics	16, 17, 18, 19, 20, 21, 22, 23, 24, 25	
Writing Performance		
Skill	**Items**	**Skills for Reteaching**
Writing Form	Writing Prompt	

Performance Summary continued

Unit 4 Unit Test   Date Administered _____

Reading Skills Performance		
Skill	**Items**	**Skills for Reteaching**
Comprehension Skills	1, 3, 4, 6, 9, 11, 13, 15	
High-Frequency Words	2, 5, 14	
Vocabulary Strategies	7, 8, 10, 12	
Phonics	16, 17, 18, 19, 20, 21, 22, 23, 24, 25	
Writing and Grammar Skills Performance		
Skill	**Items**	**Skills for Reteaching**
Grammar	2, 3, 4, 5, 6, 7, 8, 10	
Spelling	1, 9	
Writing Form	Writing Prompt	

Unit 5 Benchmark Test   Date Administered _____

Reading Skills Performance		
Skill	**Items**	**Skills for Reteaching**
Comprehension Skills	1, 4, 6, 7, 9, 12, 14, 15	
High-Frequency Words	2, 3, 11, 13	
Vocabulary Strategies	5, 8, 10	
Phonics	16, 17, 18, 19, 20, 21, 22, 23, 24, 25	
Writing and Grammar Skills Performance		
Skill	**Items**	**Skills for Reteaching**
Grammar	1, 2, 4, 5, 6, 7, 8, 9	
Spelling	3, 10	
Writing Form	Writing Prompt	

Unit 6 Unit Test   Date Administered _____

Reading Skills Performance		
Skill	**Items**	**Skills for Reteaching**
Comprehension Skills	1, 2, 4, 8, 9, 12, 14, 15	
High-Frequency Words	3, 6, 13	
Vocabulary Strategies	5, 7, 10, 11	
Phonics	16, 17, 18, 19, 20, 21, 22, 23, 24, 25	
Writing and Grammar Skills Performance		
Skill	**Items**	**Skills for Reteaching**
Grammar	3, 4, 5, 6, 7, 8, 9, 10	
Spelling	1, 2	
Writing Form	Writing Prompt	